Xamissa

Poets Out Loud

Elisabeth Frost, series editor

Xamissa

Henk Rossouw

Fordham University Press   New York   2018

Fordham University Press has no responsibility for the
persistence or accuracy of URLs for external or third-
party Internet websites referred to in this publication
and does not guarantee that any content on such
websites is, or will remain, accurate or appropriate.

Fordham University Press also publishes its books
in a variety of electronic formats. Some content that
appears in print may not be available in electronic
books.

Visit us online at www.fordhampress.com.

Library of Congress Cataloging-in-Publication Data
available online at https://catalog.loc.gov.

Printed in the United States of America

20 19 18   5 4 3 2

First edition

for Jared, Chad, and Tavia

Contents

Proloog

In 1990s Cape Town, in the interregnum after the fall of apartheid, the poet Sandile Dikeni created "Monday Blues," the city's first desegregated reading series, at Café Camissa on Kloof Street. Sandile, who had trained himself to write in his head while under detention without trial, read his work, his telegraphs to the sky, from memory. Perhaps it was here the urban legend emerged: "Camissa," we thought, meant "place of sweet waters" in the indigenous Khoe language. And the waters the urban legend speaks of have run from Table Mountain to the sea, under the city itself, since before the Dutch ships. An untrammeled toponym, from before the 1652 arrival of the Vereenigde Oostindische Compagnie (VOC), "Camissa" became a wellspring for the cultural reclamation I witnessed in newly democratic Cape Town. In the 2000s, Café Camissa shut down to make way for a real estate agency—a symptom. Ubi sunt, Sandile?

Turns out "Camissa" was a linguistic error: Colonists likely mistook the Khoe words for water, freshwater, to mean an actual place. Still, its legendary springs and streams exist—I have gone down into tunnels on the mountainside, waded in the underground water, surfaced from a manhole almost at the sea. And the echo of its promise, of the nascent city it names into being, haunts us—on the double album *Dream State*, the jazz composer Kyle Shepherd recorded the track "Xamissa." Its X stands for, in part, the multiple ways in the intersecting languages of Cape Town, past and present—Khoe, |Xam, Afrikaans, Xhosa—you may pronounce the first consonant.

"By 1660, all the major language groups of the world . . . were represented in the windswept peninsula near the southernmost tip of Africa," writes Robert Shell. For most, the polyglossia of early Cape Town was involuntary. The VOC had colonized the Cape to set up a way station on its shipping route between Amsterdam and the Indian Ocean territories it had seized. From 1652 to 1808, the VOC, as well as Dutch, German, French, and English settlers, imported 63,000 enslaved people to the Cape, largely from—and regions nearby—India, Indonesia, Madagascar, and Mozambique. Mercantile antagonism between the Dutch West India Company in the Americas and the VOC—also known as the Dutch East India Company— meant that the VOC funded slavery largely in the Indian Ocean Basin. Chartered in 1602, to monopolize the spice trade, the VOC had become the first publicly traded company and its monogram—the intertwined letters V, O, and C—the precursor of corporate logos. This recurrent logo marks the first colonial structure at the center of the city: The VOC Lodge held up to 1,000 people and, until 1828, remained the "largest single slave holding"—an urban plantation—at the Cape.

I first encountered the photograph of Roggebaai, an unsegregated, pre-apartheid beach at the city center, the absence of which "The Water Archives" circles around, in the apartment of Zackie Achmat, a presiding figure in *Xamissa*. A South African activist, born in 1962 and imprisoned several times from the age of 15 on for his anti-apartheid resistance, Zackie cofounded the National Coalition for Gay and Lesbian Equality, in 1994, and the Treatment Action Campaign, in 1998, in order to confront the post-apartheid government and its fatal inertia over the HIV/AIDS pandemic. In prison, Zackie read Lorca. His memories of 1990s Long Street augment my own.

G.P.-S.

BI-25

REPUBLIC OF SOUTH AFRICA
REPUBLIEK VAN SUID-AFRIKA

E193877

PROOF OF REGISTRATION OF BIRTH
BEWYS VAN REGISTRASIE VAN GEBOORTE

THIS IS TO CERTIFY THAT THE BIRTH OF THE CHILD WHOSE PARTICULARS ARE GIVEN BELOW, WAS
HIERBY WORD GESERTIFISEER DAT DIE GEBOORTE VAN DIE KIND WIE SE BESONDERHEDE HIERONDER

REPORTED TO ME TODAY:
VERSTREK IS, VANDAG BY MY AANGEMELD IS:

Surname
Van ..... Rossouw

First names in full
Volle voorname ..... HENK

Date of birth: Day **9** Month **12** Year **1977** Sex **Male**
Geboortedatum: Dag Maand Jaar Geslag

Identity number of father
Identiteitsnommer 5 2 0 1 0 5 5 0 7 8 0 0 9

Identity number of mother
Identiteitsnommer van moeder 5 3 1 0 2 7 0 1 0 3 0 0 3

Place
Plek .....

Date
Datum .....

3 -1- 1978
BELLVILLE
REGISTRAR OF ...

(signature)
Registrar of Births
Registrateur van Geboortes

N.B.—*This document is not a birth certificate. An identity document in respect of this child will be issued as soon as possible. If the identity document has not*
L.W.—*Hierdie dokument is nie 'n geboortesertifikaat nie. 'n Identiteitsdokument ten opsigte van hierdie kind sal so gou doenlik uitgereik word. Indien die*

been received within three months from the date of issue of this certificate inquiries should be made at the Secretary for the Interior, Private Bag X114,
identiteitsdokument nie binne drie maande vanaf die datum van uitreiking van hierdie sertifikaat ontvang is nie, moet navraag gedoen word by die Sekretaris van
Pretoria 0001

Binnelandse Sake, Privaatsak X114, Pretoria, 0001.

19771209 5127 08 3 is the son of two numbers.

The first eight digits of "father" and "mother" denote respective date of birth.

The next four digits: Above 5,000 = male. Below = female.

Two isolated digits categorize "race" under the Population Registration Act of 1950.

00 = whiteness | witheid.

00 = a sickness in South Africa and.   Infected at birth. Eerste asem | first breath.

The final digit is for arithmetical control.

His number ends in 08 3. Issued: 1986. A state of emergency or emergence.

08 = category of after   the repeal of the Act above. Or,   00 there in the echo.

These numbers do not indicate class, nor sexual orientation, nor the number of times, sixteen, the above-numbered family change their street address between 1977 and

A song of after. Subject position of song incomplete

        in the city ahead

REARRIVAL

.

The loops of telephone wire   on creosote poles

copy—in dusk-lit

          sine waves—the arcade
flight pattern of the city

starlings. Red-winged, shadow-bodied, the birds

cloud the stone courtyard of the Ⅴ℄ Slave Lodge

and parking garages and eaves. This is

civil twilight. I have been absent for seven years.

Murmuration—
          collective noun for the cloudburst of starlings in the early winter sky,

my brother says. Starlings on the telephone wires line the foothill streets of Walmer Estate. Our roadside
perception of the houses and warehouses and lots, sloping toward the harbor below, has been anchored
momentarily among

the crowd on the footbridge,
once segregated (BLANK-
ES/NIE-BLANKES) with legislative
sheet metal, and now

          a suspended desire line

above Rolihlahla Boulevard—renamed for the president

imprisoned
          on the island often
visible from here.

The tarmac with his name contours against the table-shaped mountain as it bisects the city.

Xamissa vs. Cape Town, the city in the brochure, little more than
          a summer dress, all air, colour and light, cast off onto

the indigenous peninsula—like a beautiful wet bag over the mouth of.

Hoerikwaggo means, in the crossed-out language, mountain in the sea?

The Standard Bank sign on the foreshore

—cement land reclaimed from the sea and the descendants of enslaved Xamissans, who would launch slender
fishing boats there, from the shoreline now buried under rubble—

flickers on blue against the close of day.

Xamissa, the city at nightfall double-lit,
                                    by the artificial and the fleeting.

Electric sunset. The early

sodium-vapor street lamps echo the burnt orange.

※

Domestic servants leaving Walmer Estate
cross the footbridge

in their nightly katabasis downhill.
                              Shoprite bags in hand or balanced

on their heads—wages tithed to get home
to Lavender Hill, Mitchell's Plain, Lost City, Khayelitsha, Langa, Gugulethu

outside the city gates—
as the touts in the white
minibus taxis

echo the muezzin:
                  Vredehoek, Vredehoek, Vred'hoek, W-a-a-a-a-a-a-a-a-lmer.

꒐

On the footbridge, my brother and I look at the city

in silence. Daylight has not yet left

                        the avocado-green facade
of Ghazala Food & Kaffie
on the corner   the corner of   and day-glo
vies with the fluorescent-lit   shelves—

soap   matches   pilchards

stacked behind the shopkeeper at rest in the doorway, marking time until the tidal
hiss of the 102 bus. Some cross the city for his cumin samosas.

On the roads below,
      Melbourne and Roodebloem,
narrowing downhill
the stoeps on either side

      darken first.

You must be hungry, my brother says. I have aged
without him.

He lives near the abutment
of the bridge—   starlings in his attic,

and the dock cranes, new since
democracy, frame the sea as if

to lower the sun, a starboard-red
container, beyond the coastal
shelf.

The shipping line of sunlight   leaving for

In the city   begin
and begin again

sleep's graffiti

§

The city is tidal. In the day, people stream into the city to sebenza to thetha to be here by the sea. I take the bus from Philippi for over two hours to get to high school here. At night the tide of us departs and it's the umlungu city again, the sea-foam ncinci.
(Songo Tinise

I recur in the city, song-lit,

in Songo's tidal city

now a landscape, now a room   (Walter Benjamin

now the Cape, now Xamissa

—urban legend, El Dorado,

place of sweet waters? Plural
for the sake of its springs,

　　　　　the water archive

incipient on the mountainside
artesian and running

under the city　　　　asleep.

5

The city

separate as the sleep of another

§

If one were scattered at the end   from a cardboard urn
after the flood,   with a view of the sward descending
to the bights and the coves,   the sea-bitten coast

one was born far from,   one's beginning
forgotten—   a handful of South African ash—
even the ash would echo   names of water,

distant water. The Whaleback Ledge   lighthouse
across the Piscataqua,   whose origins beyond
the harbor and the tidal mouth   split into Salmon Falls

and the Cocheco, rapid foaming water,   fed by the Ela,
the Mad, and the Isinglass—   rivers striated
by glacial ice   and rising from the Nubble and the Coldrain,

ponds,   replacements?   For Xamissa, place of

THE DREAM OF THE ROAD

And so,   my father rode the devil
out of the Kawasaki   1300 c.c. six-cylinder
I'd wash Sundays.   We, the Kingdom Riders.
Colors emblazoned   on our backs:
A biker in a helmet, visor down,   riding the cross
full throttle.   Fingers clasped like studs
to his leathers,   I rode pillion,
the rest of the Kingdom Riders   a flue of black geese.

Oom Ibby,   short for Ibrahim,
converted with his girl   Jesse, who was beautiful,
from the rival Black Widows   to ride with us
on his Yamaha   behind the quixotic Kawasaki.
In the haze   of the semi-desert
Karoo   beyond the speed limit, I remember
the windmills of where I was born.
                                Jesse died young.
Tire blossomed.   The mountain pass. The valley below.
Ibby got out of hospital, lung punctured   by his rib.
We went to see him   on the other side of the city,
where his people were allowed to live.   In the pine box, without
the blue helmet   Jesse had a small head of curls.
Her mouth was shut.
                                She'd dialect
my father's name   turn Eugene into Denie
—sounds like genie.   In Afrikaans, anything
can happen.   His ouma had almost ended him,
my father, thirty years before.   She'd held a pillowslip
over his face in the crib.   Lazarus in diapers.

If my father wasn't home,   his ghost was.
I'd wrestle him   on the carpet, rough with Lego
to name me again—a nation—   if I won
and hoist me   where Jesse was
in heaven, an upended   bucket with a palace on top
ablaze like Caltex   the refinery, my night light.

DOPPLER SHIFT

On the way to the kitchen this sensation of walking again in Xamissa of the low-rise buildings the inevitable pastel of salt-desaturated paint also in motion as if walking alongside up Long Street of being in and among the city surrounded its inhabitants heading to the Palm Mosque or Lola's or the Long Street Baths simultaneous with these footsteps for a second the present now seven hours ahead—

§

In the archive a photograph of a lost earlier
image, ca. 1890, the pedestrians now a blur,

　　　now wisps of movimento.

Time's walking river is long　　　(Kamau Brathwaite

Portuguese creole, the early franca of the Indian Ocean
trade in islanders, enslaved,　　　to fund the seafoam city of Cabo | Caab | Cape
Town.

Fezzes snap-brims head scarves
　　　on the street that runs
　　　from the sea to the foot-

hills. Long Street! where
Xamissa se mense, free

for a night would find the temporary
succor of cockfights dice-games prayer.　　In the 18th C.

the Palm Mosque has two palms
and at the doorsteps of the double-

stories—flat-roofed by ordinance

in fear the Hanglip maroon polis
would again set the thatched,
　　　　　iniquitous city　　alight

—plank bridges lead across the sluit,
a shallow low-walled canal, and now

I walk on Long Street in double-time, at the speed of water, spring water, a

water archive entry,
its alacrity diverted
under the sidewalk,

the canal absent since the belle epoque gas leak　　exploding, circa

⹖

Xamissa's chronotope—

  the middens of black
  mussels whose eaters

  cross-hatch ochre
    and begin, lithic,

subsistent   a city in a sea-cave.

A *city of corporations*   (George Oppen
   and the grassland before

transhumant pasture

extrapolates itself
from potable water.

A city of storms—Adamstor

fails in *The Lusíadas*
to drown its advent.

The scorbutic arrivals canalize
or cannabalize Xamissa, a city

of streambeds cicadas stony pines quartzite.

The streets emerge
beside the canals

BuitengrachtBuitensingelBuitenkant

outside canal outside crescent outside
side and the Dutch outsiders separate

land from water   rights.

The canals are buried
water? Time's ossuary

in a city imposed upon
shell middens, littoral,

a city unsanctioned

now—   Royal Dutch Shell

ζ

Eina! in Afrikaans taken
from the Khoe language—

    Ow!

In exchange for trade wind
Capetonians return
the city to its first name
at night, Xamissa,

to a language of dilapidated stone

crosses. Smallpox? Small game?

The sea dark

♪

       In the 90s, ek sê,   I knew

two street kids, Ashraf and Stix

flâneurs of small change and half-eaten KFC

       who'd aanklop the café tables on Long St—
       kanala kanala—where time's walking river

is. Descendants of forced movimento over the sea?

The kids peroxide their afros

orange—the shade of sodium-vapor lamps.

Street life's about walking   (Ashraf

Ja, they call us strollers   (Stix

Strollers obsessed with cars.   One time

I gave Stix and Ashraf a driving lesson
       in the cable car parking lot above
the city hoping to keep them okay
       next time they hi-jinxed another
late-model Mercedes.

Knock before you come in   (Ashraf

about to doss outside in the doorway of Salon Capri.

Kanala kanala, they would say, echo
of canal or a loanword from Malay?

Please or do me favor, Zackie tells me
       it means: A plea for hospitality, a signal
that we may eat at the same café table

in the shadow of Table Mountain.

Stix was run over.   No-one knows where

Ashraf is.

FOLDING SCREEN

Twin Soldiers

My brother and I grew up with wind   in Richwood
starter homes constructed   on the sands

amid the refinery and the oil depot   a neighborhood of beige
storage vats and bungalows   the column of fire

above the flare stack   perpetual, burning off
the excess.   The plume of smoke was a weather vane

for the southeaster   ushering, over the sewage farm
and the closed racecourse   the methane out to sea.

Hidden in the coppice   in the vacant lot, opposite
the home we avoided   he and I dug a pit inside

a Dunlop tractor tire discarded in the sand   and covered it up
with hack-sawed tree limbs.   I was the oldest, by seven minutes,

the foxhole his idea—   he would crouch there, glasses off
and watch the shadows   of the restless acacia leaves.

Without the windblown sand to pumice us,   down in the foxhole
we could play gin rummy   on top of the pilfered toolbox.

I had discarded the screwdrivers   to stash my cap guns in there
and his asthma inhaler   for the instant, in the night often

the wind swiveled northwest—   pulling the methane like a blanket
over us.   If he asphyxiated

I'd go AWOL   from the foster home
of the foxhole. I made him overdose   on his inhaler

burst after burst   until his skinny frame
in threadbare pajamas   shuddered with the medicine.

The Prisoner

Recall the waves   the color of rust as the sun descends
behind Robben Island   on the coastal selva oscura
grasses wild on the nuchal dunes   until I can almost enter

the porous sea-house   the manse to my uncle's church
mortared with quicklime   damp walls osmotic
at high tide   and, on Sunday, wake up there

and see Gugu again, older   in the leopard print
she had slipped into   after seeing her mom, who lived at the back,
sweep the church.   I invited her to the cellar

to see the relics I had found   intact, buried in the lime.
Gugu liked their names   pear whelk, paper fig,
calico scallop, and   hidden under grey polyester shorts

the sjambok welts on my backside   from the whipping I'd got
for taking a ball-peen hammer to the mortar   ancient, irreplaceable
made of burnt shell   brine-slaked in the lime kilns

on the beach nearby.   In the cellar, I showed her the evidence.
I told her   I had been looking for hollows
with the ball-peen, for the secret   —like I'd read about all winter—

souterrain that would take us   under the seabed to the island, the island
we could barely make out   when she led me to the cellar window
salt-spangled   to glimpse the bright coast there.

The island has a prisoner   she confided
like my Count of Monte Cristo   who quarries limestone
with a sledgehammer.   Did she know the wind

would lift her leopard print?   Gooseflesh, until

                              Gugu's mom lost her job.

Elegy for the Gesture

I was the sea-foam kid   bruises on my face
with a school tie   copied from the British
and knotted like a garrote.   Seamount Primary was segregated then.

Rush hour traffic   ran over my shadow;
I let an empty hand drag   against the cyclone fence
along the roadside, the median strip oleanders   perforated with light

I couldn't keep. The camera   my father gave me—
with his thumbprint   on the lens I had left there
and the dent in the body   from the time the police took it

at the funeral, before   opening fire on the crowd
the camera with the light meter   he let me figure out, in silence
on second weekends   the camera I'd taken

to school, to be like him   and document the kids
who donnered me   —the camera broken and clogging
the locker room urinal.

And the cooling towers   of the distant power station
issued shadow like a sundial   as a truck, crowded with black men
standing on the flatbed   crossed Ascot Road—

men in azure coveralls, picks and shovels at their feet   faces ashen.
They were holding onto each other   for balance. I was artless
then. I ran behind the truck   and I copied the boy

in the *Argus* photograph   my father had taken
the boy my age   at the graves of his friends in the resistance
who raised his fist   above the stones, as if holding onto

the air, and   I was seen by the men
in my school uniform, fist aloft   and the men copied me.

THE WATER ARCHIVES

Above the city, leopard clouds—

       rosettes of imminent rain on the bright.

The crowd on Adderley St de-thronged
and fishless since

      the absence of the sea
in downtown Xamissa.

Roggebaai Beach haptic
          unsegregated open

until sand legislated into concrete, water into avenue.

      Beach Street | Strand Straat
      now a mile from its referent.

Demolished, *now a landscape, now a room*   (Walter Benjamin
      under the verandah. The crowd walks through

      the broken room of Anna

      and Louis   van Mauritius—leader

        in the uprising of
    —her beloved.

At his trial, in 1808, Louis

predicts Rolihlahla @ Rivonia: *I had heard that in other countries*

all persons were free, and there were so many black people here who could also be free, and that we ought to fight for
our freedom and then, basta!
        (Court of Justice 516, W. Cape Archives, 1808

Xamissa, the code-switch
        of time?

The sea's erasure: run-up
act of apartheid to expel

black leisure. Axe the un-
segregated beach with
banks, highway, a sealed

harbor—

      now the fishless crowd sways to the second line of the distant sea.

    ⸮

In a blink—0.0001 of a day

—my brother and I alight

      from the Golden Arrow bus

into a monkey's wedding | a sun shower

      in the city of iKapa, semi-
clouded, the leopard another guest.

Among the tidal
      convo, the delta
of pedestrians

my brother and I are morphemes

in the sentences of the city. Uthini? Eish, I sold my skorokoro. And the mayor, that sell-out tief, I'll kak on the
doorstep of her gentoo palace, right by the nice brass knocker. J'ai marché plus de mille kilomètres pour arriver ici.
Heita da! Sharp-sharp. Jislaaik, the larneys are mos taking over alles now. Aweh, hoesit? Duidelik.

Xamissa is   sprachbund, city of utterance

and creole echoes, none more Xamissa than

      the dialectic of now-now and just now—

now-now, a little sooner than soon, not right now, I'll be there now-now

just now, an indefinite time in the future, you shall be freed   just now.

The glint of abalone at the bottom of the reissued canal that leads to the Waterfront
      mall,

of the twelve rixdollars
per month,

Anna, free, must pay
Louis's eienaar until

just now;   justice.

§

On crutches, my brother. Slow, we

cross the eddy of Adderley St.   Flotsam advert-
isements TEKKIE TOWN | Sneakerville   ATLAS
FINANCE   and someone inside the CASH 4 GOLD
sandwich board   snap-snaps her finger
against the handbill to catch

our attention in the rain, letters blotted. On the
          jaundice-yellow map, its photocopy
damp in my bag, the early Cape crowded with

watercourses and canals.

The urban legend—that before the Dutch

ships, the Cape was called

          Camissa, *place of sweet waters*—

no more than a colonial lisp.

In Khoekhoegowab, Nama, remnants
          now spoken in the desert to the north:

||àm̋-mi, water |'áà-sà, fresh, new.

Eish! Xamissa not a place but water itself,

archival, open as the city in May
when the streets are water again,

now and again?   Xamissa, partially free, sidewalk wrinkled

in the people-streams, my brother and I

attached molecules—he the other H in our double bond, covalent, the crowd
          on the street our O.

Cities are the contradictions of capitalism, spelled out in crowds

(Adam Gopnik

My brother works for Louis.
In the echo of uprising on
Strand St. To reclaim his city

not from the sea but the 𝒱𝒸

꙼

Feral rain. The flood light seeps through the curtain

in my brother's spare
bedroom. Sans
sleep—

>   The farm where Louis begins
>   the uprising called Vogelgezang,
>
>   Birdsong. One of the last streets
>   left with its name in District Six.
>
>   During the trial, Anna dies of—

I gaze again, on my cellphone,   at Roggebaai.jpeg.

The bright, fish-laden boats.   In the image, the scintillant

Roggebaai water.   Strand Street un-stranded. Domestic, interior,

Table Mountain
for eating under

and angular   as Garlics
Wholesale Warehouse.   Nets of dresses and rolled-up hems. The crowd

reflected in the damp sand   —Louis and Anna among

the distant waves just now—a liminal city   afoot on the seabed for

a tidal instant, without   abelungu | white foam.

Like Chaplin in *Modern Times* ended the era of silent comedy with the cicatrix
        of song   , so too am I trampled

now-now

by your exodus, O
crowd of Xamissa.

I part the muslin curtain   and witness, as if *The Flying Dutchman*

              a late bus—destination Lost City.

HELENA | LENA | ᐸᘁᐱ

The pages that follow depend upon a 1727 archival record, which suggests that a figure named Lena van de Caab, without precedent in her lifetime, marooned from the urban plantation of the Lodge to join a city of her making in the mountains beyond Cape Town and that 14 women and men, soon after, echoed her action.

Writing at a distance from the city of my birth, I first encountered her name in a digital list of hundreds of Lodge occupants in the 7,500 page e-book *From Diaspora to Diorama: The Old Slave Lodge in Cape Town*. To make primary sources easily available to ordinary South Africans, the historian Robert C.-H. Shell and a team of researchers transcribed as many documents as possible from the archive relating to the VOC's hand in slavery at the Cape.

"helena | Lena | ⟨∿∿⟩" began in the aftershock of reading the words "Occupation: Runaway" underneath her name in the digital 1727 Lodge census. I returned to Cape Town. Holding over 1,000 feet of material relating to the VOC's subjugation of the Cape from 1652 to 1795, the Western Cape Archives lay behind the Victorian-era facade and high stone walls of the infamous prison it had replaced on Roeland Street. With assistance from archivist Erika le Roux, I located the census on paper—only to find that Council of Policy volume 2449 was not a census but an inventory: In 1727, during Governor Jan de la Fontaine's transfer of power to his successor, the VOC had ordered a complete "stock-take" of its possessions at the Cape, from furniture to gardening tools to human beings.

The VOC kept track of enslaved people in far greater detail than its employees—likewise, no equivalent database lists the many burghers upon whom the slave trade depended. In the handwriting of a nameless VOC functionary, who listed in the inventory the names of enslaved people at the Lodge, I recognized by implication my own hand in the document. I named the functionary Pieter Fourie, after my grandfather, as a proxy figure both for myself and for my Huguenot ancestors, French immigrants eager to benefit from slavery.

The archival trace of Helena van de Caab is fragmentary at best—by definition, the VOC records precluded her speech. In addition to the 1727 inventory, further records name her: the show trial in 1730 of over a dozen people convicted for joining the Hanglip maroon community, which included a "Lena van de Caab," and the individual trial of a person of the same name and age in 1737. Robert Ross calls these records "the 'material deposit' left by the exercise of judicial terror at the Cape." While the VOC often assigned both the first name "Helena"—Lena is the contraction—and the generic last name "van de Caab," to indicate an enslaved person born in captivity, "of the Cape," in the archive's 18th-century records there is just one person so named who took flight from the Lodge.

How did Lena's name become ᨒᨊ? A handful of documents archived as "legal evidence," which enslaved Bugis-speaking people from Indonesia had written in an ambiguous script—lontara—interrupts to this day the dominant language of the archive, Dutch: VOC employees could not read lontara and viewed it as a threat to their power. Instances of lontara in the poem can be seen both as language resistant to the VOC and as placeholders for Lena's own words, suppressed from the archive. In that spirit, I have sometimes transliterated her name into lontara. Translations of the script are on page 111.

In financial dire straits, the VOC became defunct in 1799 after the short-lived Batavian Republic nationalized its assets. Great Britain took over the Dutch colonies, including the Cape, in the Napoleonic Wars, by which time the moral bankruptcy of the VOC and the person-owning society it fostered had laid the groundwork for apartheid. Still, the Hanglip maroon community lasted until emancipation in 1834—someone chiseled A PERSON FREED into Table Mountain, on the pathless route that Lena would likely have taken more than one hundred years earlier.

May my head not split, may my mouth not tear. I ask permission first to put it on paper. It should not be forgotten.
(Sureq Galigo

The Ⓥ¢ on the brink

of bankruptcy

.

            Its gutted shell
company remains—

the Cape archive kept the facade
of the Roeland Street prison, its

instituting imaginary   (Achille Mbembe

The portcullis opens onto

corridors and stack rooms. Urns

of corporate ash

.

In debt,   a debtor, I sit at Table 5 near
a door open to the courtyard garden—

                a former employee by birth.

I write the debris number C 2449 on the form

in pencil and wait for the ash in the half-light

Ƒ

pellejanis
Maniiane
tengamis
toemoele
Elisabeth van Mateke₈

Weggelopene Slavinne

helena van de Caab 1725. in maart
Loelassis van rio de lagoa 2 Jan: 1727.
henguanes ———— ₫ . 2 d₀ d₀

₩₩ 233 en daaronder 5 bandijten,

Council of Policy   (C 2449

[ash transcript]

Monster rolle van soodanige Slaven, banditen en Slavinnen, als in Weesen bevonden zijn, onder ult. febr. 5 1727—

Weggelopene Slavinne

helena van de Caab 1725. in maart
Loelaffis van Rio de la Goa 2 Jan: 1727
Henguanes _____ 2 J: _____

5

In Dutch *monster* translates into both monster and muster.

I address U, helena van de Caab. An after-song.

The V̄C̄ list U almost last in the 1727 inventory—employee Pieter Fourie tallies its armaments, furniture, gardening tools, and teaspoons in the Governor's house, in the selfsame volume.

The Company cannot count U,   Lena. U are not here.
In secret U write in lontara, the four-corned letters U learn in the ⁓˙o madrassa?

U maroon in March, 1725. Two years later, Loelaffis and Henguanes echo yr action.

To translate the inventory heading *Weggelopene Slavinne* as "runaway female slaves"
re-inscribes the Cape, the rigid city U flee or set on fire, ⟨⁓⌃.

Is it not "run-toward"? To run toward each other,   three lives, three women,

helena, Loelaffis, Henguanes.   To run toward the other city U construct.

⌇

U are the hero? helena van de Caab   1725. in maart

The ~~muse~~.

The strikethrough cannot erase the fact that I listen not in silence but in song, a form of interruption. Song in Dutch is *lied*. Past tense   to lie?

Does yr existence, in the Dutch-sick documenten, silence one second of invocation since the Homer-system? Does the patina of this hand on the rag-paper

re-silence U? Is yr resilience discounted if

this asker becomes reliant on U, ⟨∿⌒

—the end of apartheid predicated upon
the future U construct   on foot?

If not a muse, if not a metonym for resistance,
then ∿⌄⌒? I re-iterate your name out of time.
Below the Lodge cellar, where perhaps U sleep in late summer—on the eve of marronage—

runs an iteration of ⁄⁄⌄o

               the streambed

               archival   underground

ξ

Lena,

by whose hand are U itemized—yr absence
from the inventory of 1727—in these goose quill

curlicues? Whose blots the ink with sand? Each

yellow page framed in cardstock and stitched

into the torso-size

volume C 2449.   Legible ash

.

Perhaps an ancestor of mine
Pieter Fourie a functionary

and minor son who does not
inherit the farm in the interior

who does not own
anyone and wants

to. The misspellings (cf. slavinne)   the ornate script
the willingness to please—of the nascent
                        burgher   his kin Huguenot émigrés

.

I inherit his fleshy cheekbones, his Y
chromosome, his shoe-size, his shoes

his benefits.   Pieter is the spit-image of Oupa, blotto,

my Oupa who works for the Post Office, in a blankes-
alleenlik   position his entire—until
cirrhosis of the liver, as if the dry sand of Pieter Fourie

still trickles from the volume   to suppress fire, to blot out

∮

If my hypothesis is
correct, the primary
function of writing   *is to facilitate the enslavement of other human beings.*

(Claude Lévi-Strauss

⚡

U maroon from the iron Lodge, the urban plantation. helena van de Caab

1725. in maart   —*marronerons-nous?*   (Aimé Césaire

The limewash facade of the Lodge, blinding in March
light,   delimits the systemic city, as if   Cabo | Caab | Cape
Town rises within its stone courtyard: The white repeats

itself citywide—the Houses
of Parliament, the High Court,

the Library—all of which fail to   wall U in
.   Lena, none of this   is the city

    if U are the center.

The Cape in yr lifetime almost   ash.
The Cape in yr lifetime almost   garden

again.

ƻ

[alternate take]

I step out of the crowd into
        Shoe Archive on Main
for the SALE written in red
        on dust-streaked glass.
Threshold: white-washed
        pillars and an iron bell
hanging from the arch.
        Displayed on pine boxes
the shoes I own
        North Star takkies, tire-
tread sandals, Pepstores
        schoolboy shoes, Hi-Tecs,
diachronic   worn-out
        and taped on the drywall
the yellowing placaat
        —such penmanship—
forbidding the slaven, slavinnen
        van de Caab to own
whatsoever shoes
        in the city of excrement.
Through the shop glass
        clouds of ash-edged
paper billow and float
        in the heat—on fire, the
Ѱ document storage
        warehouse on Roeland St.
Heretofore unseen:
        a piece of census again
or a ship's manifest
        redacted with ash and
doubt.   At the threshold
        onto the arson street

the iron bell clinks
        in the shop doorway.
I stumble and pause
        to remove my Adidas
as if I had the right
        even to yr blisters—

ʑ

To begin again at the source of the city: The iron

Lodge, windowless in yr time, helena

van de Caab. If yr last name were no longer Dutch-

given, if U chose a name in the instant of marronage: Lena

van ⁀⌣o, Lena van de Stilte,

⌇⌇ of   —would yr first name be silence also, or if

this paper vigil outside the Lodge, in the late summer

wind, were to beckon U to the air slit on the stairwell

U would signal—shut   up—with an ashen finger

to yr lips?

⌇

The **V̸C̸**, a joint-stock LLC.　　　Limited liability—

easier to find the line item
of yr name　　helena van de Caab 1725. in maart

than the names of the Heren XVII
　　　Dutch board of directors, who profit from

.

Shareholders vote by a show of hands.

Here, this hand

open on the page

ϟ

5/25/2016   I read the inventory again   in search of yr city.

〈∿∿, I see what I want to see, a narrative—

U the hero—first in the dates of marronage?

[ash transcript]

Weggelopen Slaven   Council of Policy (C 2449

Jouda	1725 in Julij opgedrost
francois van Mallebaar	1725 in October
Imaika	den 3 [Aug] 1726
Sitaij	"18 [Aug] _____
Cupido van de Oust.	"20 Junij 172[7]
Saisa	"6 Septt. 1726
Guajemanus van Rio de la Goa	21 Xbr 1726
Pambaij alias, Pane Ifasÿ	29 [Aug] 1725
Winkohouw	Jan 1726
Nicodemus	Jan 1727
Alexander	[Aug] 1726
Rengen van Madure	20 Febr. 1727

Weggelopene Slavinne

helena van de Caab	1725. in maart
Loelaffis van Rio de la Goa	2 Jan: 1727
Henguanes _____	2 J: _____

⚡

It is in the nature of beginning

that something new is started which cannot be expected from whatever may have happened before. This character of startling unexpectedness is inherent in all beginnings. . . . The fact that [↽∿⌣] is capable of action means that the unexpected can be expected from [her], *that* [she] *is able to perform what is infinitely improbable. And this again is possible only because each* [∿⌣∿] *is unique, so that with each birth something uniquely new comes into the world.*

(Hannah Arendt

⚡

Born in 1699?

U are ~26 years old when U begin—the first in yr lifetime to maroon from the iron

Lodge. helena van de Caab 1725. in maart.

Not in yr words—a Dutch account. It was late summer.

Yr future companions at the Hanglip polis

maroon from the far-flung Company farms, but none until U from the Lodge itself,
the urban plantation at the Cape, epicenter of the Dutch settlement.

A narrative. In yr lifetime, ⟨∿↷⟩, yr action becomes a path for the women and men above

named? In the months to follow, after U begin

the nascent city of ⁄⁄∨o, its citizens maroon,   fourteen in all, and

↯

first a word U resist? For instance

, the $\mathcal{VC}$ the first

pre-industrial company to
issue shares. Average annual
profit at the time of
yr birth as a line item
2 million guilders—

and if the citizens, ∿̌

follow U in the impossible
hope U will look back, if
not at the new city then at
yr foot-prints—about to be
precedent, path?   U begin

, helena van de Caab   1725. in maart.

U begin

⫽∿̇o,

a new entry in the water archives? A new entrance?

foot prints are usually easy to see, but foot steps . . . are often difficult to trace

(Clare Anderson

⸘

ᨉᨗ,

in the absence of U

I read Dutch

court records
as if   echo-
location
          .   [ash transcript]

          Ik heb op
de wonde
          op de Boegi-
neese wijse
          gespuuwt

| I spat on the wounds in the Buginese way.   (September van Bougies, CJ 373

September, actual name unknown, seized from the archipelago   Sulawesi Island

ᨉᨈᨛᨅ, a literate healer and letter recipient. His spit perhaps

dangerous as ink to the Dutch.

The letter in his chest, folded small. The address

ᨆᨛᨚᨊᨑᨈᨉᨆ | This is a letter to brother September in Platte Kloof
ᨅᨈᨆᨚᨉᨈᨅᨈᨂ
ᨓᨊᨆᨗᨈᨉᨈ

I touch the red wax. The folds in the shape of a childhood house.

Inside, his friend ᨈᨗ ᨊᨚ iterates

the word for person 23 times.

          (CJ 373, a rare

          instance of anti-
          Dutch

or Bugis abugida
amid
the voluminous

.

The existence of the letter
from ᜋᜒᜈᜓ to ᜂᜒᜈᜒᜎᜒᜎ

enough [medium = message]

for the ♀ Court
of Justice, of mot juste
to sentence

September van Bougies to

ᜥ

Wat sê jy, Lena?

If not nothing. Inside
a city of silence.

I denied U the agency of flesh

, left out
a love—

      Jochem [van de Caab]

murdered in 1729?

If action is speech (Hannah Arendt
there's nothing of U in this archive
          van mijne.

⸮

The city has been garden before

    amid the myriad waters.

Through knowing grasses   *time slips*   (Aimé Césaire

The before-people, foragers, garden with fire—

    tend the fynbos to reveal the iris-
family geophytes, tasty watsonias and gladioli.
    The shrublands
come back after rain, gracile

  ⚡

In the archive I pencil
the end U run-toward
on the mountain lip if

.

The employers of Pieter Fourie

insist the city begin
with a Company

fort or garden—

[Signed] Leendert Janz, N. Proot. Amsterdam, 26th July, 1649.

⸗

Would like to have some slaves for the dirtiest and heaviest work, to take the place of the Dutchmen in fetching stone, &c, . . . Forgot to ask in former letter for some Batavia vinegar— consider it cheaper than Dutch.

[Signed] J. v. Riebeeck. Cape of Good Hope, 25th May, 1652.

⸙

〈⌒⌒, the city U begin

exists in name

　　　∥⌄o

the instant their iron-
bell economy invests
in lime trees to cure
leuenaars of scurvy?

[Signed] a militia of liars

∫

I talk to U on paper, ‹∿∧. New lies
on paper. On the verso: guesses

, leading questions. U are forced to work in the Company Garden for a time?

Or the Company kitchen, where U take the flint on the mantel?

helena van de Caab. 1725. An ashen finger to yr

lips. In one version of events—   a song to begin ∥✓o

          —U set yrself   and the city alight.

ξ

A fake reckoning if

I insist U are silent.

The silent hero

of "helena | Lena | ᘇᕽ"

, the founder of Xamissa
—a city that is not here?

I need U mute | muse
in order to
sing to U?

The umlungu lullaby

The water archive, in the echo of.　　　After-song.

Our mothers tell us we should not throw stones at the swallow,
//kabbi-ta-/khwa. *It is the rain's thing.*　　　　　(Dia!kwain

　　　In my time, in yr time, water
　　　runs beneath the city, Lena, to migrate

from the sea as if　　　swallows　　　swallows　　　swallows
overhead, a flight

southbound. The sea-vapor clouds the flat
　　　mountaintop, its eponymous
tablecloth, and returns to water against
　　　the cool stone and the grassy, low

fynbos, to trickle back to the city, under
its avenues sloping seaward, and it feeds

　　　the well inside the cobble-stone courtyard
　　　of the Lodge, a blessing in summer, and in

winter, *a demographic sinkhole*　　　　　(Robert Shell

　　The cellar where the newest

　　　　　　　Pellejanis　　(C 2449
　　　　　　　Manuane
　　　　　　　Tengamis
　　　　　　　Toemocke
　　　　　　　Elisabeth van Matekes

　　sleep—where U begin?—

flood-prone

　⚡

Lontara omits

consonant twinning, the glottal stop, and the last velar nasal. *For instance,*

ᨅ

may be read as pa, ppa, pang, ppang, paq, ppaq (Roger Tol

In Bugis, ᨕᨅᨅᨈ

has at least two
referents, *élong, éloq*
song and love

and ᨅᨚ is both
beautiful and sand—

ambiguity and poly-interpretability are built-in characteristics of the script.

Lontara signals a section-break with

᨜

If, on the stone lip
of the Lodge well,

U haul up the archival

in an unreliable
bucket, ⟨∿∿⟩,

would U scrawl the new
⟨∿∿∿⟩ in water lontara?

.

Bugis, an ambiguous—

○෴ is either *sara/ng*

sorrow or bird's nest

.

The swallows have gone

    and U begin

and begin again

○෴, a two-syllable

song, left to evaporate, late summer

1725. in maart?

෴

Oral instance of ⟨∿∿∿⟩

—ten generations after

1725. in maart—

Zackie Achmat, a Xamissan
activist, in solitary for

1976-era arson
before the age of sixteen,

relates this link:

to keep him safe, his mother

fastens against his skin
a paper talisman, a jimat

just like (jislaaik)

this one in the Cape archive   (CJ 424
, silent lontara folded inside

not in the first place meant to be read, but to be carried on the body   (Koolhof and Ross

Wat sê jy,   Lena?

ᶚ

In the paper archive I read Dutch-sick. In double-time

I stand outside on the median strip that
      divides Heerengracht, outside
the iron Lodge in the seaward wind, the glass city

salt-lit. ⟨∿∿,   how long have U been awake?

    Being is self-sufficient   (Édouard Glissant
        whereas every question is

interactive. I ask questions U don't ask for—to become
        porous as limestone. To not
              asphyxiate in the inner room
of the archive, which my people, Company employees,

itemize U in, or is it
      silence I ask of U?   On stilts of

whiteness   paper-thin, a witness

I look up at the second floor   —where U are?

And the crowdsong—the kids of color heading to Cape Town High, my father's alma, at the top of the Company
Gardens—school me to my feet

  ⌇

Halfwassen Meyden & Schoolkinders: Caabse   (C 2449, 1727

Margriet	van	Maria Been
Dorotea	"	Wollemangij
Cornelia	"	Sophia van Angij
Jannetje	"	Sabina van Mallabaar
Anna Margriet	"	Maria van Mente
Margriet	"	Sophia Angij
Elisabeth	"	Marretje van Fatimo
Anna	"	Pennewouw
Lea	"	Orbelase
Elisabeth	"	Christijn Pieters
Elisabeth	"	Ramahefta
Adriana	"	Maria Blom
Elisabeth	"	Martje van Mente

ξ

If the water archive has no work song is yr first thought

on the eve of marronage

1725. in maart

an anticipated sip of ⁄⁄ⱴo

or of fire?

⌇

Pieter Fourie is the first

to burn

ʑ

The iron Lodge. The city's initial structure

and longest surviving.   Lena, in a version of the time to come I stand outside

          its seventh iteration.   The stucco emblem in the pediment

made by re-named artisans—Malay-speaking,

          or perhaps Malagasy, or a language of Rio de la Goa, Mozambique? Could the artisans

speak to U, ⟨◠◠, or U to them? The stucco

repeats the Ⓥ logo. In the beginning was. The iron serif and overlapping letters

signify the clink of

ș

In the summer wind, the city's south-
        east blade, tinnitus recurs—as if an inner

ear now traps another cicada. ⟨∿∿⟩, the closest

I have come to rupture   of privilege—

the summer night in 1999 the home-made
bomb an eight-inch galvanized steel pipe

crammed with fertilizer
perhaps and shrapnel

seeds an instant
corn field on fire

and throws me from one end of the barroom to the other.

Subject position—

I open my eyes to
companions licked

by flame and our eardrums
flaps of skin as if
opened with a screwdriver.

The doors, blown off, reveal the sidewalk and swirling

blue lights outside

⌇

The kitchen Dutch
word   luister

—the sibilant of -st-
I struggle to hear with
tinnitus and it is also

the abbrev. of street

on which basis—the city
U begin?—I attempt to

stutter toward U   into the wind
between us.   Lena, the bomb
displaces me seven or eight
feet.   To say I am that
much closer to U transliterates
        a silence into nothing but abyss?

Traumatic reaction is not the only form of resistance   (Édouard Glissant

Underground—   in the water archives—
        U spit on yr wounds
in the Buginese way?

I ask U at the margin of the city U begin again

in silence a form of

ꞩ

Lena, perhaps

      the wind says

I am the constant
bomb U de-arm

and tinnitus is my ₵ name in yr ear

.

In the wind-version U are not even here.

To begin with

ᵴ

And the wind oscillates
       the oak leaves as if

Government Avenue—
       tree-lined and soon

on fire—were saying
       bye, ⟨∿⌢. Burn us.

≶

Clouds of ash-edged paper billow and float in the heat—on fire, the

DEPOT   KAB
SOURCE   CJ
TYPE   LEER
VOLUME_NO   786
SYSTEM   01
REFERENCE   16
PART   1
DESCRIPTION   LENA. VAN DE CAAB. VONNIS.
STARTING   17370000
ENDING   17370000

Each sentence I utter to U another lash?

⚡

〈∿∽, in yr time the Lodge
has a single iron key taken

away at nightfall to seal

the quarters—prototype
of the city—into a vast

hecatomb in case of
arson, mass immolation

⚡

And Pieter's fear of arson is one reoccurrence in the urns of corporate ash—

there was a plot formed by some fugitive slaves to set the town on fire; they began in the South Eastern corner so as to take advantage of the prevailing South Eastern Wind, which was likely to fan the flames, and set fire to a shoemaker's workshop

(O. Mentzel, *Life at the Cape*, 1736

Fire drafts the architecture

       of the VC city. The flat roofs
       and the firebreak alleys—

ordinance of corporate panic.

Fire, the first
resistance to

this.

꿍

We shall watch   (Steve Biko
as time destroys
     his paper castles

and know that all these
little pranks were but   frantic
attempts of frightened

little people to convince
each other that they can

control the minds and
bodies of

.

Is it time, Lena?

⚡

Without gloves, I hold the ashen paper up to the half-light. The $\mathcal{VC}$ watermark.

   Pieter Fourie likes to embellish

the sentence. From his hand to mine.

ξ

Alsoo uijt de vrijwillige
gerecolleerde Confessie van Jena
van de Caab Slavin der Comp:
oud 38 jaaren, thans 's Heeren
gevangene, en andere Stukken ten
Proresse gefourneerd, den E Achtb
Raad van Justitie des Casteels
de goede hoop Sonne klaar is gebleecken

The sentence I write re-inscribes
its iron end, helena van de Caab?

The sentence

en gebrandmerkt en vervolgend wederom in de ketting geslaagen zijnde, dus daar inne als
bevoorend haar leven lang te blijven

(CJ 786 ref. 16, 1737)

The city of ends

if U end
up here?

I vomit paper

castles. I cannot keep water down.

Water, water is a mountain   (Gertrude Stein

If the water archive were both 〰〰,

Lena, the city would burn and begin?

.

If the sentence is not inevitable, to see the beginning and not the

〉

If U are the center, Lena,

     the city's fate incessant, open-

ended, a delta archived underground

.

Table Mountain, that more or less
liberated zone which looked down
on the Dutch city of Cape Town   (Koolhof and Ross

〈∿∿, at night through the iron Lodge air-slit U see

     the camp fires of resistance, kin, abundant
     on the mountainside,   as if another

version of the future is visible, a palimpsest city

unpaved?

The mountain—once the source of the city's water

ξ

helena van de Caab 1725. in maart

    To begin the urban is to be among?

Loelaffis van Rio de la Goa 2 Jan: 1727
Henguanes _____ 2 J: _____

    who follow U to the mountain lip

, the fire escape

ϟ

In the archives of ⁄⁄˙o, according to a stream, arson ends the Ṽ₵. From the Lodge cellar, damp underground, U emerge unhurt. Maroons descend the mountain—citizens also. The ships give up. The click-sounds of Khoe thicken the new creole, its letters now cousins of lontara. In the account you write, of your life in ⁄⁄˙o after the ash, you speak to your readers, your descendants, of the tinder: At the time of the shoemaker's workshop fire, U could not, by law, wear

ʑ

If yr time, Lena, were

a forked stream, are U among

> Pellejanis
> Manuane
> Tengamis
> Toemocke
> Elisabeth

van Matekes, in head scarves,
linen bundles aloft, on foot

ahead of me on Government
Ave, alongside the Gardens,

yr diet vitamin-empty, despite
the vegetable reasons

for the Dutch city—the ash
version—in the first place?

Yr white scarf, if so,

loosens in the southeaster

⚡

An urban spring underground
        —the Cape gardeners

who leave for U, at the verge,

hidden in the split
stony pine, a cache

: naartjies, grapes, limes, melon,
barley—enough to summit—

and who carve ⁄⁄˅o in the bark

.

The gardeners

had their gathering places in the gardens of this Table Valley, which are just above the houses of this settlement, as a
result of which, no doubt, sad accidents of fire—

                                    (D. van den Henghel, CJ 340, 1736

To maroon is to be among, Lena,

unmet companions left behind?

⁄⁄˅o, the word-of-mouth city U taste until

1725. in maart.   The gardeners feed

U with their whispers?

Follow, in the late summer, the water archives—
now a trickle—backward and up the mountain.

⸌

〈ᔈᔈ,

if the 18th century Dutch word buchu

archives the Khoe for the fragrant
genus *agathosma*   in the citrus family

whose seeds demand altitude
and long flames to germinate

.

if the scent of buchu on the slope
above   signals the city U begin

        almost there, almost underfoot

.

        if the loose maps—begin and begin
again—of maroon routes trace

the forked water in late summer, up
        into the mountain, a palimpsest

stream papered over, then

ᔊ

The ꝟ on the brink of

fire-erasure from the Cape,

in the five years U are among
the maroon polis Hanglip   in the mountains

above the Dutch

.

And U come back to burn

the city, the Lodge, any ⟨∿∿∿
toward U. The paper castles

U torch?

Pieter Fourie   ashens inside.

Bugis U burn and yr name and thirst

itself—∥ˇo also.   Only yr subsequent
footfalls on the slope upward has a sound

at all?

subsequent | səbsəkwənt |

(of a stream or valley) having a direction or character determined by the resistance to erosion of
the underlying rock, and typically following the strike of the strata

ɕ

On the way up   the Capelsluit to the Platteklip
stream, feet blistered,   I tell the mountain

the next city will be   the door sequence
of these Lodge-style bungalows   flung open

instead of sprinklers, dogs, and armed
response signs   leading to the last
parking lot in   ᵠ₵ Park, where the slope becomes

wall. Fynbos on the face of Table Mountain purchases water in the cloud arcade supplemented by occasional
rain and the result cannot linger on the steep catchment agglomerating into springs filtered by 3558 feet of silica
one of which hidden by foliage joins a subterranean stream as it emerges from the mountainside and irrigates the
transhumant summer pasture of the previous and for this water the trade wind sailors choose this variable bay rife
with north-west storms that replenish the Platteklip which slows down to a dribble in March a month and a name
assigned in order of descent from the gangplank March van Rio de la Goa April van Rio de la Goa forcing the
water carriers of the Cape to climb up here unshod when the well on Greenmarket Square runs dry and among
others

⟨∿⌃, have U had to pound linen on the cascaded

boulders until Platteklip translates into flat stone?

⌇

par de savantes herbes le temps glisse   (Aimé Césaire

〈⌒⌒,

if U look back U would burst into flame?

Each footstep another nail in the forehead
of the acting governor Jan de la Fontaine

and Pieter Fourie, employee of the month

.

                    The mountain grasses olive and gracile

⌇

A crack in the sheer mountain
face, a shaded kloof or couloir

and the heat dips
in the height above sea level.

helena van de Caab. 1725. in maart

U follow its sound, the stream
invisible under the ericaceous

.

The water archive, its streambed, vanishes
back underground. Silica and sedimentary
rock steepen into brink. Time to eat, as if
for the first time, a kind of freedom, Lena?

Perhaps U peel a naartjie

—from the Tamil for
tangerine, nārattai—

as cicadas whir. The buchu
in the kloof a sensate green

.

A first meal in the city U begin?

In the distance U hear the dogs

ξ

above the Large Cloud the Table Mountain, celebrated at the Cape of Good Hope because of its table-like appearance and principally for a white cloud, which covers it at the approach of a violent south-easter

(Nicolas-Louis de La Caille

.

In the wind-version,

    in the white cloud

    of privilege or ash

    no paper attempt

    may locate U, ⟨∿⌃,

no male invoke/yoke U.

ƻ

On Table Mountain U write
〷 ọ in the sand?

The water archives recur.
The mountaintop earlier

a riverbed   —and the cliff
polis of Hanglip, a granite wave
in the distance,   pale blue

.

Water, water is a mountain
                    (Gertrude Stein

     ⸕

I see what I want to see. An ashen narrative. In the archive

U find the maroon polis   on False Bay's opposite arm

under the aegis of Leander ܀ ܀ܘ   the leader at Hanglip

who sends former captives back to burn the Cape several

times & who, in the pendulum year of 1737, almost poison

the Dutch water source, the Platteklip, at the flat stones

on which free companions, yours even after

yr sentence, balance like a city for another hundred

years, arms out?

܀

To maroon is to be with? To be among

Adam, Christina, December,   Fortuyn, Dina, Perra, Caesar,

       Eloris, January, Aron,   Anna, Marthinus,

Lijs, Alexander, Mars,   Batjoe, May,   Arend, Joumath,

ᚷᚾᚾ, Jochem, Cupido,   September, Rosetta, Amil,   Leander,

Philander, Barkat,   Diana, Titus, Scipio, Pieter, November,

       Anthony, December, Meij,   Venus, Cupido, January,

Sara, Joseph, Colon, Pieter,   Toesina, Simon, Alexander,

       Loelaffis? Henguanes?

ᚥ

Blisters lanced by stone I stumble

. Daylight shelved   now-now

in the archive of the night.

          I gaze up at the mountain—

yr footfalls a sonar in the city ahead

helena van de Caab.   1725. in maart

.

I vote with opened feet toward U

Lena, until

Lontara Translation

Lontara	Transliteration	Translation from Bugis to English
ｨｖo	Ka.Mi.Sa	*Xamissa*. Approximation in Bugis.
ｃｍｎ	Le.Na	*Léna*. Lena, or Helena van de Caab.
ｎｖ	Pa.Da	*Pada*, "equal, same, together."
ｎｖｎ	Pa.Da.Ta	*Padatta*, "person, fellow human being."
ｃｍｎｎ	E.Lo	Either *élong* or *éloq*, "song" or "love."
oｎ	Sa.Ra	Either *sara* or *sarang*, "sorrow" or "bird's nest."
ｉ o	Ke.Si	Either *kessing* or *kessiq*, "beautiful" or "sand."
ｎｎo	U.Pa.Se	*Upas*, author of 1760 letter addressed to September.
oｃｎｎｎ	Si.Te.Be.Re	*Sitémbéréq*, or September, recipient of Upas' letter.
ｎｎ o	Bu.Gi.Sa	*Bugis*, the last name of Leander, the Hanglip leader.

Sources

Primary Archival Sources

The following volumes from the Western Cape Archives and Records Service, in Cape Town, were invaluable in the writing of *Xamissa*: C 2449; CJ 424; CJ 785; CJ 786; CJ 373; CJ 516.

Images

The images on pages 36, 49, 66, and 92 are courtesy of the Western Cape Archives and Records Service and sourced from S80; C 2449, p. 135; CJ 786 ref. 16, p. 113; CJ 373, pp. 141–142.

Secondary Archival Sources

Nigel Worden and Gerald Groenewald, eds., *Trials of Slavery: Selected Documents Concerning Slaves from the Criminal Records of the Council of Justice at the Cape of Good Hope, 1705–1794* (Cape Town: Van Riebeeck Society for the Publication of South African Historical Documents, 2005); George M. C. Theal, *Chronicles of Cape Commanders: Or, an Abstract of Original Manuscripts in the Archives of the Cape Colony* (Cape Town: W. A. Richards, 1882); H. C. V. Leibrandt, ed., *Precis of the Archives of the Cape of Good Hope, December 1651–December 1653: Riebeeck's Journals, etc.* (Cape Town: W. A. Richards and Sons, 1897).

Quotations

Claire Anderson, "Subaltern Lives: History, Identity and Memory in the Indian Ocean World," *History Compass* 11, no. 7 (2013): 503–507; Hannah Arendt, *The Human Condition* (Chicago: University of Chicago Press, 2012), 177–179; Walter Benjamin, "On Some Motifs in Baudelaire," *Reflections: Essays, Aphorisms, Autobiographical Writings* (New York: Schocken Books, 1978), 156; Kamau Brathwaite, "Islands," in *The Arrivants: A New World Trilogy* (New York: Oxford University Press, 2005), 120; Steve Biko, *I Write What I Like: A Selection of His Writings* (Johannesburg: Picador Africa, 2004), 79; Aimé Césaire, *Aimé Césaire: The Collected Poetry*, trans. Clayton Eshleman and Annette Smith (Berkeley: University of California Press, 1983), 91, 368–369; Claude Lévi-Strauss, *Tristes Tropiques*, trans. John Russell (New York: Criterion Books, 1961), 292; Édouard Glissant, *Poetics of Relation*, trans. Betsy Wing (Ann Arbor: University of Michigan Press, 1997), 145, 161; Adam Gopnik, "Naked Cities: The Death and Life of Urban America," *New Yorker*, Oct. 5, 2015; Achille Mbembe, "The Power of the Archive and Its Limits," in *Refiguring the Archive*, ed. Carolyn Hamilton et al. (Boston: Kluwer Academic Publishers, 2002), 19; Otto Mentzel, *Lebens-Geschichte Herrn Rudolph Siegfried Allemanns . . .* (Glogau: Günther, 1784), in English *Life at the Cape in Mid-Eighteenth Century*, trans. Margaret Greenlees (Cape Town: Van Riebeeck Society, 1919), 100–101; Gertrude Stein, *Tender Buttons: The Corrected Centennial Edition*, ed. Seth Perlow (San Francisco: City Lights, 2014), 45; D. van den Henghel, CJ 340, 1736, trans. Worden and Groenewald, *Trials of Slavery*, 137; Louis van Mauritius, Western Cape Archives, CJ 516, 412.

Key Texts on Slavery at the Cape

Gabeba Baderoon, "The African Oceans—Tracing the Sea as Memory of Slavery in South African Literature and Culture," *Research in African Literatures* 40, no. 4 (2009): 89–107; Jackie Loos, *Echoes of Slavery: Voices from South Africa's Past* (Cape Town: David Philip, 2004); Robert Ross, *Cape of Torments: Slavery and Resistance in South Africa* (Boston: Routledge and Kegan Paul, 1983); Robert C.-H. Shell, *Children of Bondage: A Social History of the Slave Society at the Cape of Good Hope, 1652–1838* (Johannesburg: Witwatersrand University Press, 1994); Robert C.-H. Shell, comp., *From Diaspora to Diorama: The Old Slave Lodge in Cape Town* (Cape Town: NagsPro Media, 2013), pdf e-book; Nigel Worden, "Armed with Swords and Ostrich Feathers: Militarism and Cultural Revolution in the Cape Slave Uprising of 1808," in *War, Empire and Slavery, 1770–1830*, ed. Richard Bessel, Nicholas Guyatt, and Jane Rendall (London: Palgrave Macmillan, 2010); Nigel Worden, Elizabeth van Heyningen, and Vivian Bickford-Smith, *Cape Town: The Making of a City* (Cape Town: David Philip, 2004).

Key Texts on Lontara, Bugis, and Khoekhoegowab

Wilfried Haacke and Eliphas Eiseb, *Khoekhoegowab Dictionary with an English–Khoekhoegowab Index* (Windhoek: Gamsberg Macmillan, 2002); Sirtjo Koolhof, "The 'La Galigo': A Bugis Encyclopedia and Its Growth," *Bijdragen tot de Taal-, Land- en Volkenkunde* 155, no. 3 (1999): 362–387; Sirtjo Koolhof and Robert Ross, "Upas, September and the Bugis at the Cape of Good Hope: The Context of a Slave's Letter," *Archipel* 70 (2005): 281–308; J. Noorduyn, "Variation in the Bugis/Makasarese Script," *Bijdragen tot de Taal-, Land- en Volkenkunde* 149, no. 3 (1993): 533–570; Roger Tol, "Fish Food on a Tree Branch: Hidden Meanings in Bugis Poetry," *Bijdragen tot de Taal-, Land- en Volkenkunde* 148, no. 1 (1992): 82–102.

Other Sources

Mikhail M. Bakhtin, *The Dialogic Imagination: Four Essays*, trans. Michael Holquist and Caryl Emerson (Austin: University of Texas Press, 2014); Timothy Brook, *Vermeer's Hat: The Seventeenth Century and the Dawn of the Global World* (Toronto: Penguin Canada, 2013); Luis de Camões, "Canto V," in *The Lusiads*, trans. William C. Atkinson (New York: Penguin Books, 1952); Jan de Vries and Ad van der Woude, *The First Modern Economy: Success, Failure, and Perseverance of the Dutch Economy, 1500–1815* (Cambridge: Cambridge University Press, 2010); Ian S. Glass, *Nicolas-Louis de La Caille, Astronomer and Geodesist* (Oxford: Oxford University Press, 2012); Christopher Henshilwood et al., "Emergence of Modern Human Behavior: Middle Stone Age Engravings from South Africa," *Science* 2954, no. 5558 (2002): 1278–1280; Nelson Mandela, *Long Walk to Freedom* (New York: Abacus Books, 1995); Simon Pooley, *Burning Table Mountain: An Environmental History of Fire on the Cape Peninsula* (London: Palgrave Macmillan, 2015); Neil Roberts, *Freedom as Marronage* (Chicago: University of Chicago Press, 2015); Kerry Ward, *Networks of Empire: Forced Migration in the Dutch East India Company* (Cambridge: Cambridge University Press, 2012).

Notes

9 *Rolihlahla*: The Xhosa first name of Nelson Mandela, which means "pulling the branch of a tree," or more colloquially, "troublemaker."

10 *crossed-out language*: Refers to Khoe, a language family indigenous to the Cape, largely obliterated in the Dutch colonial period, 1652–1799.

14 *Songo Tinise*: Teenage housing rights activist in the "Reclaim the City" campaign. The quotation is a précis adapted from a personal interview and newspaper accounts. In Xhosa, *sebenza* means "work"; *thetha*, "talk"; *umlungu*, "white person"; and *ncinci*, "tiny."

19 *Oom*: Afrikaans for "uncle," used as a sign of respect toward an older person.

19 *allowed to live*: Under apartheid-era racial classification, "Coloured" meant people of mixed race, whose assigned living spaces on Cape Town's fringes were segregated under the Group Areas Act of 1950 not only from so-called "White" people but also from people designated as "Black."

24 *Cabo | Caab | Cape Town*: In the 15th century, the navigator Bartolomeu Dias rounded the southern tip of the African continent to try to circumvent the overland trade route from Europe to Asia. The Portuguese king João II named the peninsula, on which Cape Town is situated today, Cabo da Boa Esperança in anticipation of the profits from securing this trade route by sea. After the Dutch colonial occupation, in the 17th century, the spelling of Cabo shifted to Caab.

24 *Xamissa se mense*: Afrikaans for "Xamissa's people."

25 *Adamstor*: A figure invented by Luis de Camões, in his 1572 epic poem, as a mythological giant and *genius loci* of the Cape, in the shape of a storm cloud, who tries to prevent the Portuguese from circumnavigating southern Africa and establishing a seagoing trade route to India.

25 *scorbutic*: Affected with scurvy, a disease stemming from vitamin C deficiency, common among 17th century sailors. The VOC used the threat of scurvy as one justification to build a colonial fort at the Cape, in order to provision their trade ships with fruit and vegetables.

28 *ek sê*: Afrikaans, "I say." An expression, used when the speaker seeks agreement or for emphasis, along the lines of "You know what I'm saying?" in colloquial U.S. English.

32 *Gugu*: Short for "Gugulethu," a first name in the Xhosa and Zulu languages. A contraction of "igugu lethu," which means "our pride" or "our treasure."

37 *in the uprising of*: Louis van Mauritius was the leader of the 1808 Jij Rebellion, an uprising of 300 enslaved people, whose rallying cry became the promise that in freedom former owners would no longer be addressed in the third person—in the deferential grammar of Dutch—but as *jij*, "you."

37 *Rolihlahla @ Rivonia*: In the 1963 Rivonia Trial, Nelson Rolihlahla Mandela, arrested for sabotage of the apartheid state, made a speech from the dock declaring the court itself invalid, a watershed moment in the history of the struggle. Mandela was sentenced to life in prison.

39 *eienaar*: Afrikaans, "owner."

47 *Sureq Galigo*: Bugis epic poem, also known as *La Galigo*. At over 6,000 pages and dating to the 18th century—earlier manuscripts, now lost, were even longer—*La Galigo* records the creation myths of the Bugis-speaking inhabitants of Sulawesi Island in Indonesia.

50 *Monster rolle . . . onder ult. febr. 5 1727*: Transcribed title of the 1727 inventory, in Dutch, which translates as "Muster rolls of [such?] [male] slaves, convicts and [female] slaves, if found to be in existence, below *ultimo mense* [last month] February 5 1727."

50 *Weggelopene Slavinne*: A category heading transcribed from the 1727 inventory—it translates from Dutch as "runaway [female] slaves."

50 *helena van de Caab*: The small letter *h*, instead of a capital letter for her first name, reproduces an error in the 1727 inventory.

51 *U*: Dutch for "you," in its formal, respectful sense, similar to *vous* in French.

52 *marronage*: Both the flight from slavery and the sense of community such a flight engenders.

52 *the streambed*: An underground stream from Table Mountain fed the well in the Lodge.

53 *Oupa*: Afrikaans for "grandpa."

53 *blankes-alleenlik*: Under apartheid legislation, my grandfather's job at the Post Office was reserved for him.

55 *the iron Lodge, the urban plantation*: Iron, here, is a metonym for enslavement—the Lodge itself was made of wood at first, then brick from 1669 on.

56 *shoes*: "At the Cape—even in winter—[enslaved people] were forced to go barefoot," Shell writes.

58 *windowless*: "Narrow five-inch slits with iron crossbars served as 'windows,'" Shell writes, "but most external walls had no slits at all."

58 *van de Stilte*: In an echo of Lena's toponymic last name, Afrikaans for "of the Silence."

60 *Weggelopen Slaven*: Dutch for "runaway [male] slaves." Transcription from the list of enslaved men who took flight from the VOC Lodge, alongside dates of their marronage, as recorded in the 1727 inventory. Spelling errors and abbreviations—e.g., "Xbr" for October—are kept as is. Square brackets indicate illegible dates. The list of women from the same inventory who took flight has been juxtaposed below.

64 *Ik heb op . . . gespuuwt*: The words of September van Bougies, an enslaved person known for his Bugis medical knowledge, have been transcribed from his interrogation in a 1760 VOC trial.

64 *his friend*: Upas, September's Bugis-speaking friend, also enslaved, who wrote a letter to him in lontara, which the VOC seized in 1760 as circumstantial evidence in a trial to put down a recent slave uprising. For possession of this letter, September van Bougies was executed on a cross.

66 The image reproduces the address on the verso of the 1760 letter in lontara script that the enslaved person Upas wrote in the Bugis language to September van Bougies.

67 *Wat sê jy . . . ?*: Afrikaans, colloquial, "What say you?"

67 *Jochem [van de Caab]*: Either Lena and Jochem were in an existing relationship before their marronage or they met while in flight. They were not related; likely they had the same Dutch-assigned last name because they were both born into slavery at the Cape. By the time the VOC recaptured Lena in 1730, along with a dozen other people, Jochem had been murdered, possibly in a power struggle within the Hanglip maroon community.

67 *van mijne*: Dutch for "of mine."

68 *fynbos*: Afrikaans for "fine bush." Refers to shrub land endemic to the Western Cape.

71 *leuenaars*: Afrikaans for "liars."

72 *In one version of events . . . the city alight*: Possibly, Lena took part in one of the many instances in the 18th century of people at the Cape using arson to protest their enslavement. Often, these fires were acts of marronage.

73 *umlungu*: Xhosa for "white person" or, in the sense of privilege, "whiteness."

74 *Our mothers . . . the rain's thing*: The Victorian-era government sentenced Dia!kwain, one of the few people left in the 19th century who could speak the indigenous language |Xam, to hard labor for his resistance to colonial incursion in the northern Cape. He was released into the custody of linguists in Cape Town on condition that he document |Xam. The quote is from a 2015 Iziko South African Museum exhibit on |Xam language and culture, sourced from the Lloyd and Bleek Collection, and *//kabbi-ta-/khwa* approximates the |Xam word for "swallow."

74 *a demographic sinkhole*: "Throughout the period of slavery there was a clear excess of deaths and runaways over births," writes Shell. "Replenishment was through the slave trade."

74 *flood-prone*: Enslaved people from Mozambique, who the Dutch had consigned to the lowest rung of the VOC hierarchy, were often quartered in the cellar, which was vulnerable to flooding because of the underground spring that fed the well in the Lodge courtyard.

77 *Zackie Achmat*: Zackie told me this story of his mother in the 1960s pinning a paper amulet containing Arabic writing to his clothes as a boy. His protest in the form of arson—he burnt down part of his segregated school in Salt River—took place in 1976, in the wake of the Soweto youth uprising, sparked by oppressive education policies against people of color.

77 *jislaaik*: Afrikaans expression for amazement or surprise.

79 *Halfwassen Meyden . . . Martje van Mente*: List of names, categorized by the Dutch as "Half-Grown Girls

and Schoolchildren," transcribed from the same page as that of Helena van de Caab in the VOC's 1727 Lodge inventory. The second column states the name of each girl's mother.

83 *the summer night . . . steel pipe*: Bomb explosion in the Blah Bar, Cape Town, on Nov. 5, 1999.

84 *kitchen Dutch . . . luister*: "Kitchen Dutch" is the pejorative for Afrikaans, the semi-creole that had developed between colonists and enslaved people by the 18th century. The word *luister* means "listen."

87 *DEPOT . . . 17370000*: Reproduces the digital search result from the National Archives of South Africa website used to locate Lena van de Caab's 1737 trial record. The Dutch word *VONNIS* means "verdict" or "sentence."

92 The image, from the Western Cape Archives, reproduces the first page of Lena van de Caab's 1737 verdict.

93 *en gebrandmerkt . . . leven lang te blijven*: An excerpt from the sentence that the VOC handed down in Lena van de Caab's 1737 show trial, supposedly for stealing linen, seven years after her recapture. This is the last known record of her in the archive. The Dutch reads: "and branded and continue again in the chains beaten being, thus there as before her lifelong to stay."

96 *Loelaffis . . . who follow U*: Loelaffis and Henguanes could perhaps envisage their marronage in 1727 from the Lodge because of Lena's precedent in 1725. The archive has no further details on whether Loelaffis and Henguanes reached Hanglip or any other zone outside Dutch control.

98 *head scarves*: From 1642 on, the Dutch forbade enslaved people at the Cape from wearing hats. To circumvent this law, enslaved people gradually began to wear head scarves and turbans.

99 *the Cape gardeners . . . in the bark*: The VOC struggled to suppress the enslaved people who labored in the more remote vegetable plots that belonged to Dutch burghers on the mountainside above the city. That these gardeners would have assisted Lena van de Caab in her marronage—the paths up into the sanctuary of Table Mountain crossed their turf—is speculative on my part.

102 *transhumant summer pasture of the previous*: The annual movements of Khoekhoe pastoral groups, such as the Goringhaiqua, in and out of the site of the city, before Dutch colonization.

103 *acting governor Jan de la Fontaine*: The VOC-appointed governor at the Cape at the time of Lena van de Caab's marronage who commissioned the 1727 inventory. One of the signatures at the end of the 1737 trial record sentencing Lena also implicates de la Fontaine.

Acknowledgments

Thank you to Zackie Achmat for his dreams of and for the city. Through the precedent he created in his lifetime of political resistance at the Cape, Zackie let me imagine Lena. In the research phase for *Xamissa*, Zackie also let me stay in his flat, a few blocks from the archive; I first saw the photograph of Roggebaai on page 36 at his place. I'm grateful to Zackie for his knowledge of Cape Town and its history, for the meals and long walks, and for his suggestion to show my hand, as a beneficiary of slavery, through a VOC proxy figure. Dankie, ou pellie.

I'm deeply grateful to William Kentridge for permission to use his drawing on the cover and for the kindness of Catherine Belloy at the Marian Goodman Gallery. Thank you both. Erika le Roux, key archivist at the Western Cape Archives and Records Service in Cape Town, located the 1727 inventory after fruitless attempts on my own—I'm grateful for her knowledge of lontara.

Excerpts of *Xamissa* first appeared in *The Paris Review, Blackbird, The Common,* and *Tupelo Quarterly*—thank you to editors Robyn Creswell, J. Randy Marshall, John Hennessy, and Kristina Marie Darling for their support. Thanks to Wesleyan University Press and the editors of *Best American Experimental Writing 2018* for including "Rearrival." I'm also grateful to Kwame Dawes, Chris Abani, and Johnny Temple for including a long excerpt from *Xamissa* in the chapbook box set *New-Generation African Poets: Tano,* published by the African Poetry Book Fund and Akashic Books. I'd particularly like to thank Gabeba Baderoon for her generous reading. Thank you to my editor Elisabeth Frost, for her patience and vision, to Tim Roberts and Sheila Berg of Field Editorial, and to the staff of Fordham University Press, especially Richard Morrison and John Garza.

Roberto Tejada guided and inspired *Xamissa* from first draft to last. I can't thank him enough. Sally Connolly's course on the modern long poem first gave me the impetus to begin the book. The work of translators Jen Hofer and Erín Moure shaped its poetics. I'd also like to thank Sarah Ehlers, Michael Snediker, and Daniel Tiffany, whose encouragement has been invaluable. Thank you to Rodrigo Toscano, Susan Briante, and Lisa Olstein for their unflagging support. Myung Mi Jim, Douglas Kearney, Harryette Mullen, and Adam Fitzgerald have each been helpful. Thank you to Sarah Ruden, my first poetry teacher, and also to James Tate—hamba kahle.

I appreciate the efforts of David Wheeler, my first editor, who funded a research trip back to Cape Town. Subsequent funding came from the Creative Writing Program at the University of Houston—thanks to J. Kastely. I'm truly grateful to John Newsome, for his generosity over the years, and to Imara Jones, both of whom gave advice on *Xamissa*'s politics. The presence of Theodore J. Ellenhorn first opened up the possibility of writing this book and seeing it through. My friends Ata Moharreri and Nick Rattner have been a constant joy; I'm also grateful for the company of Tyson Morgan, Selena Anderson, Erika Jo Brown, Conor Bracken, Niki Herd, Zack Martin, Daniel Wallace, J. P. Gritton, Dan Chu, and Matthew Salesses. Julian Jonker and Sean O'Toole know the terrain of *Xamissa* intimately—thank you. I'm especially grateful to my parents, Dene Rossouw and Carol Dawes. Donna Lee, Gary Goldstein, and Luke Lee-Goldstein offered true support. I couldn't have written this book without my brothers, Jared and Chad Rossouw, whose activism and artwork gave rise to much of *Xamissa*. I offer this book with love to Tavia Lee-Goldstein.